My Happiness Journal

Jo Taylor

Dover Publications, Inc.
Mineola, New York

What makes you happy? You might say your family, your friends, your pet, or a hobby that you enjoy. In this fun activity book, you'll find plenty of ways to think about and describe your own happiness. There's a weekly Happiness Diary where you can list some events that made you happy, a "happy to help" coupon, and pages that invite you to describe a dessert, a book, sports, movies, a color, a song, and many more things that make you smile. Get ready to write, draw, and color as you discover just what makes YOU happy!

Bibliographical Note

My Happiness Journal is a new work, first published by Dover Publications, Inc., in 2016.

International Standard Book Number

ISBN-13: 978-0-486-80028-8
ISBN-10: 0-486-80028-8

Manufactured in the United States by LSC Communications
80028804 2018
www.doverpublications.com

About Me

My full name is ______________________________

I like it when people call me ______________________

If I were famous, I might call myself ________________

I was born on ______________ in the year __________

I'm in Grade ___ at ________________________ school

Besides me, my family includes ____________________

____

____

and we live in _______________________________

These people make me smile every day!

These people make me smile every day!

IF A GENIE APPEARED AND OFFERED TO GRANT ME THREE WISHES, MY WISHES WOULD BE...

1. ______________________________

____

2. ______________________________

____

3. ______________________________

____

Happy? Write a **'Welcome'** message.

Cut around dotted line and hang on your door

Not happy? Write a **'Keep Out!'** message here.

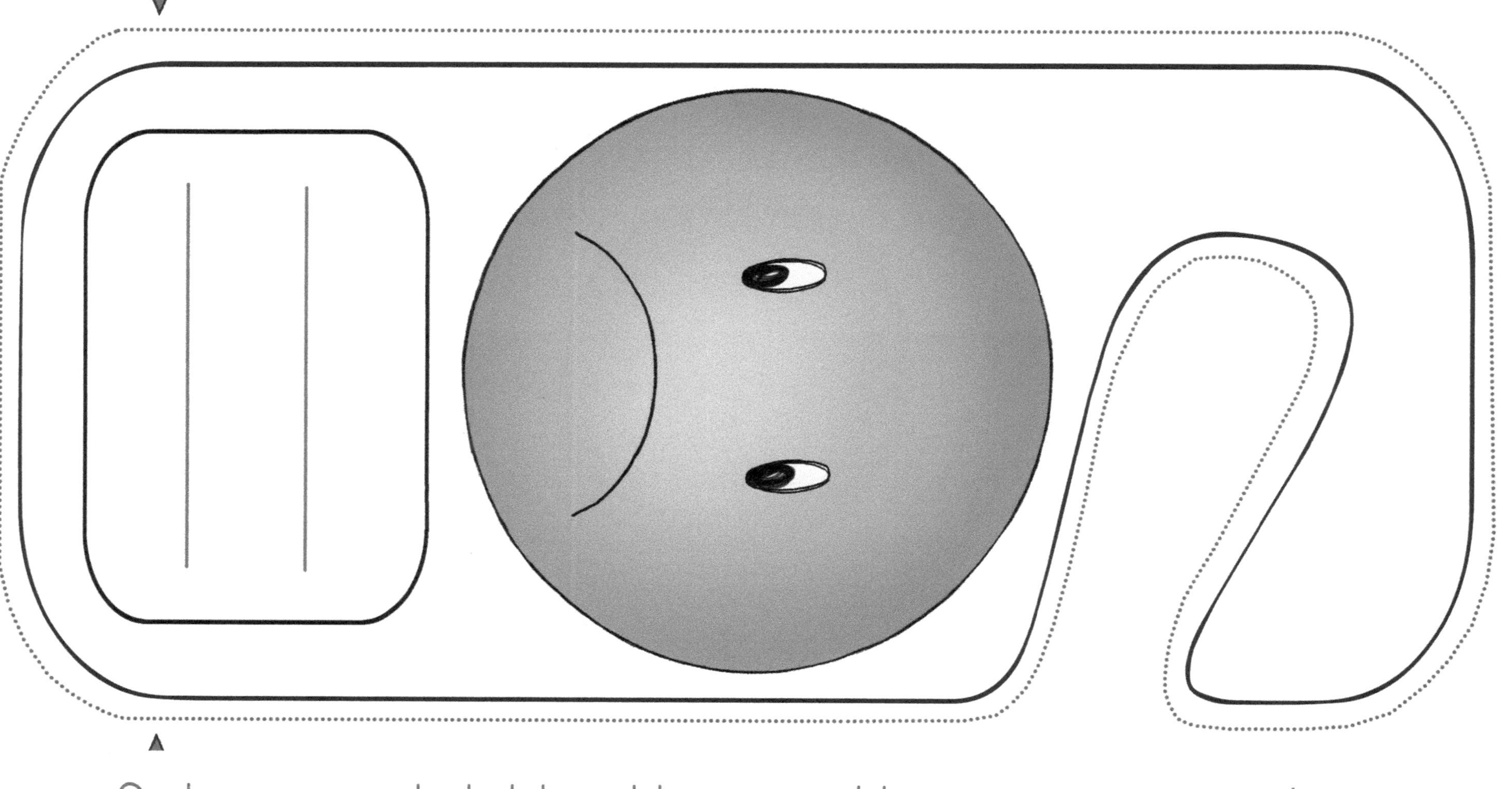

Cut around dotted line and hang on your door

Pair these with the coupons on the next page.

To ______________________________

Present this coupon and
I'll be happy to help you with

____

____

From ____________________________

To ______________________________

Present this coupon and
I'll be happy to help you with

____

____

From ____________________________

Cut on the dotted lines, fold, sign and give to someone special

...makes me
Happy!

This dessert is happiness:

Watching this sport makes me happy

Playing this sport

____

____

makes me even happier

When i was younger
this book always made

When it comes to movies, these films put a smile on my face!

WEARING MY HAIR LIKE THIS MAKES ME HAPPY...

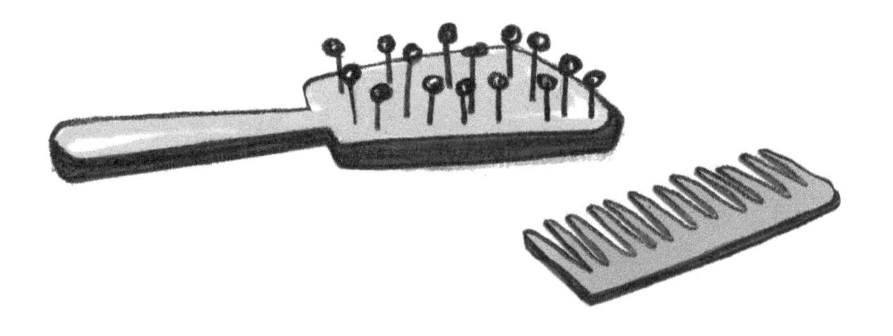

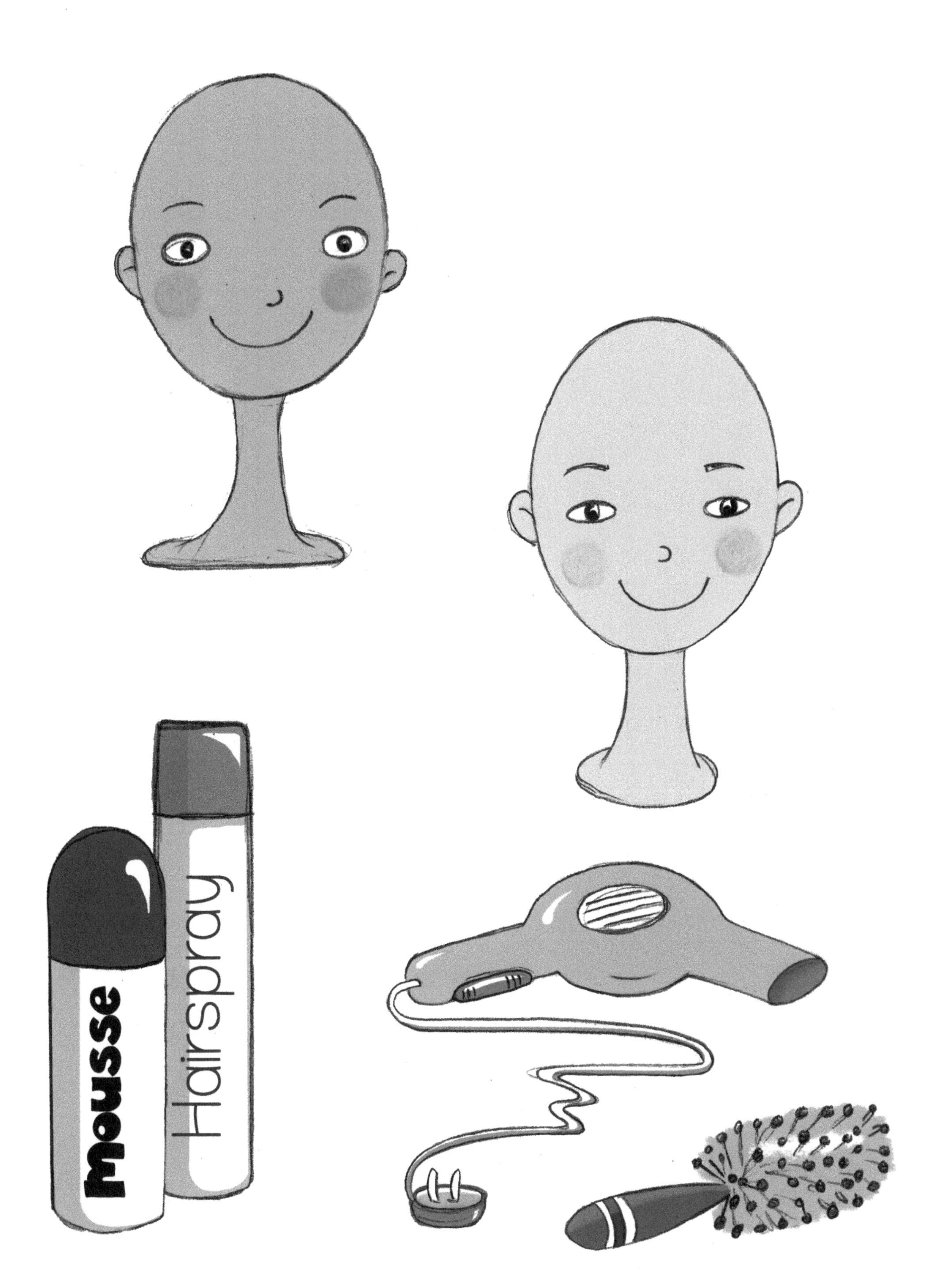
Mousse
Hairspray

Wearing certain clothes makes me happy

Here are some of them ...

Dear
You made me happy today because

My Happiness Bag!

I couldn't do without these 5 things

1. ______________________________

2. ______________________________

3. ______________________________

4. ______________________________

5. ______________________________

My recipe for Happiness

Other than my birthday, this holiday makes me happiest

Smells that make me happy

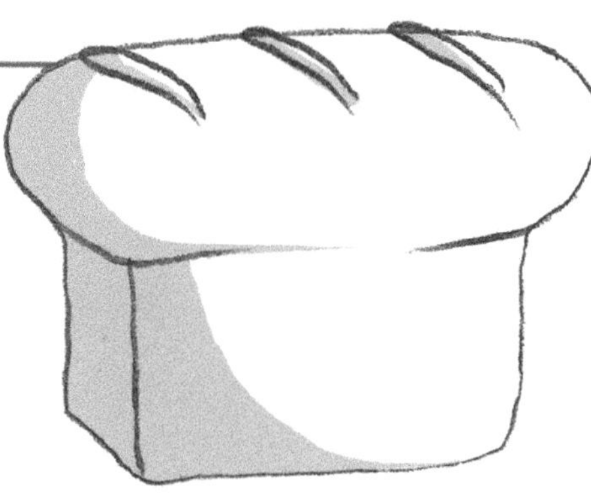

POP
Corn

Some other words for

The happiest day I ever had in school was when ...

Sneakers like this
would give me happy feet:

Here's one design

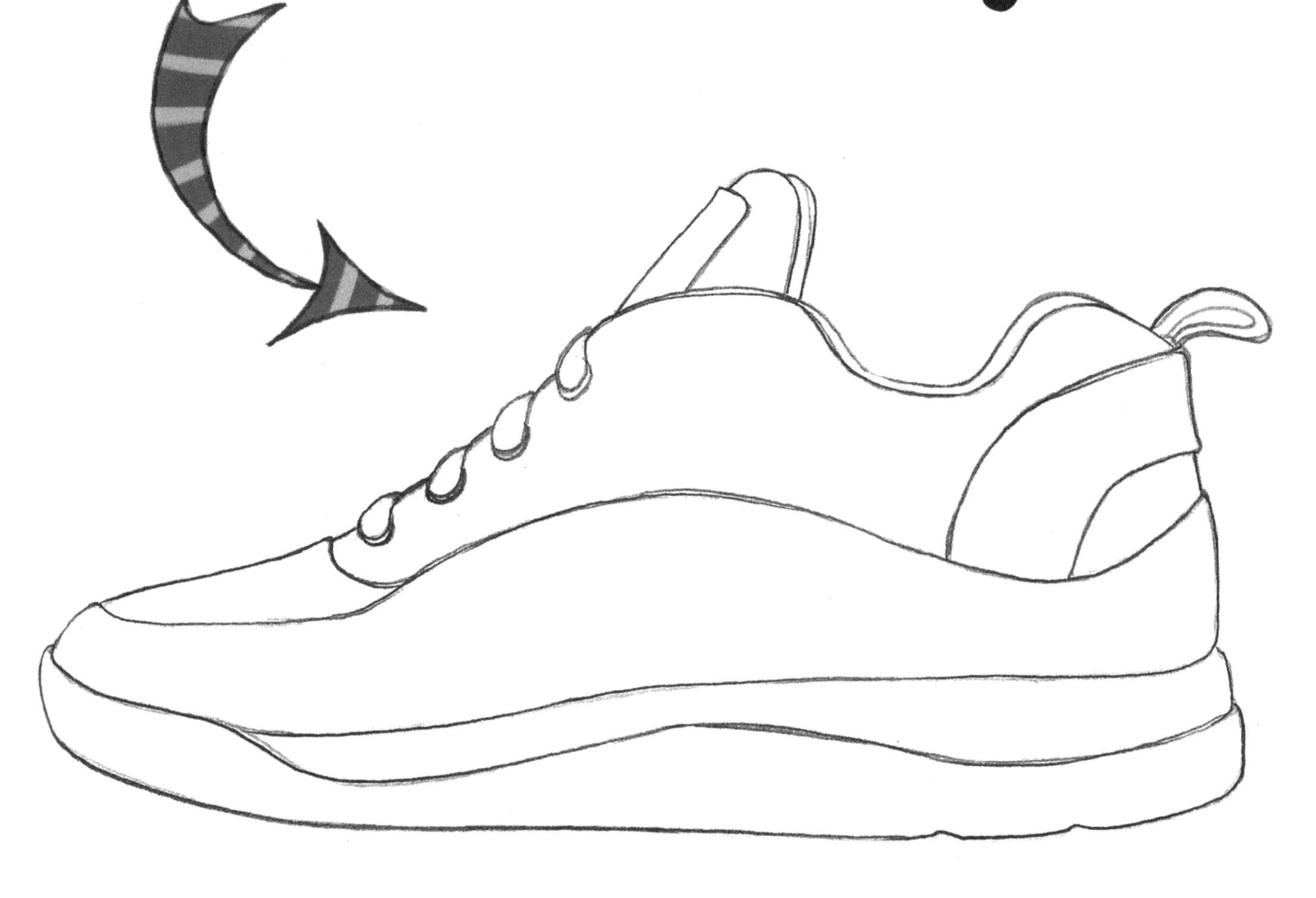

Here's another

If I'm ever feeling down, these foods can always cheer me up ...

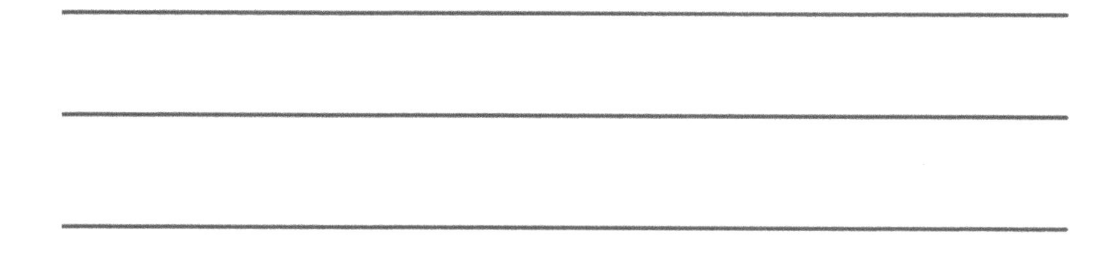

The season of the year that makes me happiest is ...

If I could live anywhere else,

I think I would be happy in

If I'm ever in a bad mood, hearing this song makes me happy.

If life gets too serious ...

I can always count on

to make me

If my favorite restaurant offered to name a menu item after me, I'd want them to call it...

Ingredients

The United Nations International Day of Happiness is celebrated on March 20th. It's a day when millions of people from around the world share images of what makes them happy.

Here's a picture of something that makes me happy!

It's not worth a lot of money, but owning this makes me very happy...

My Birthday was great this year because...

My favorite time of day is ___________

because .....

At the end of a rainbow
I'd love to find

____

____

____

Design a happy pattern
for this mug:

Friends make me happy!
I think what my friends like about me is:

Exercise can make people happy!

I like to do these things to stay in shape...

Giving this gift

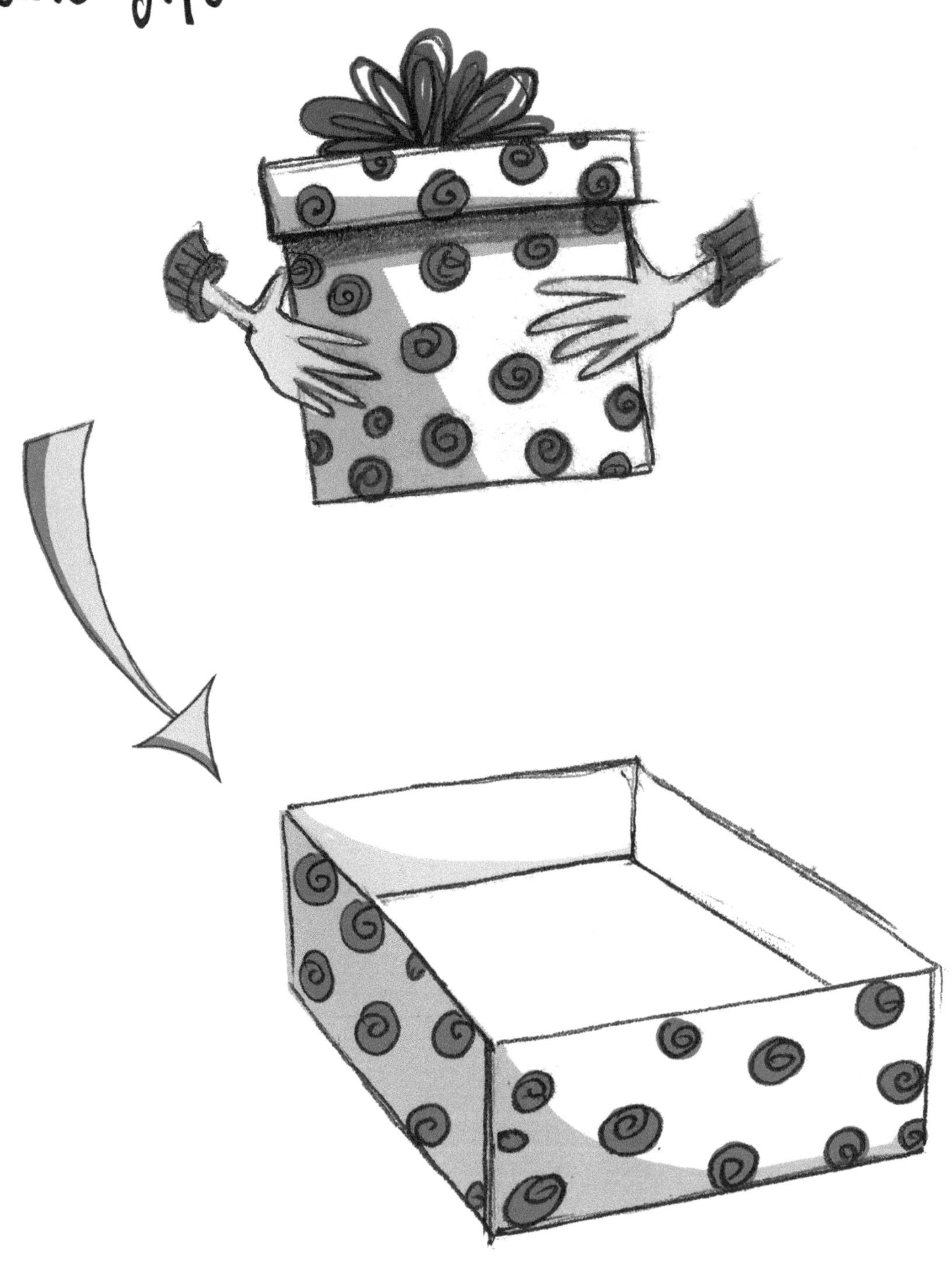

made ____________ and me happy.

Happiness is the color ____________

Here's a

that always gets a good laugh!

Here's a drawing of my best smile

I am a Good Friend

because ....

I am always happy to get a text from

I felt like a winner when ...

I would smile all night

with these three famous people ...

1. ______________________________

2. ______________________________

3. ______________________________

I would be really happy to have a pet ________________

Things to do if I'm having a bad day

1.
2.
3.
4.
5.

My Happiness Diary

Happy things happen every day!
Here are some that have happened to me...

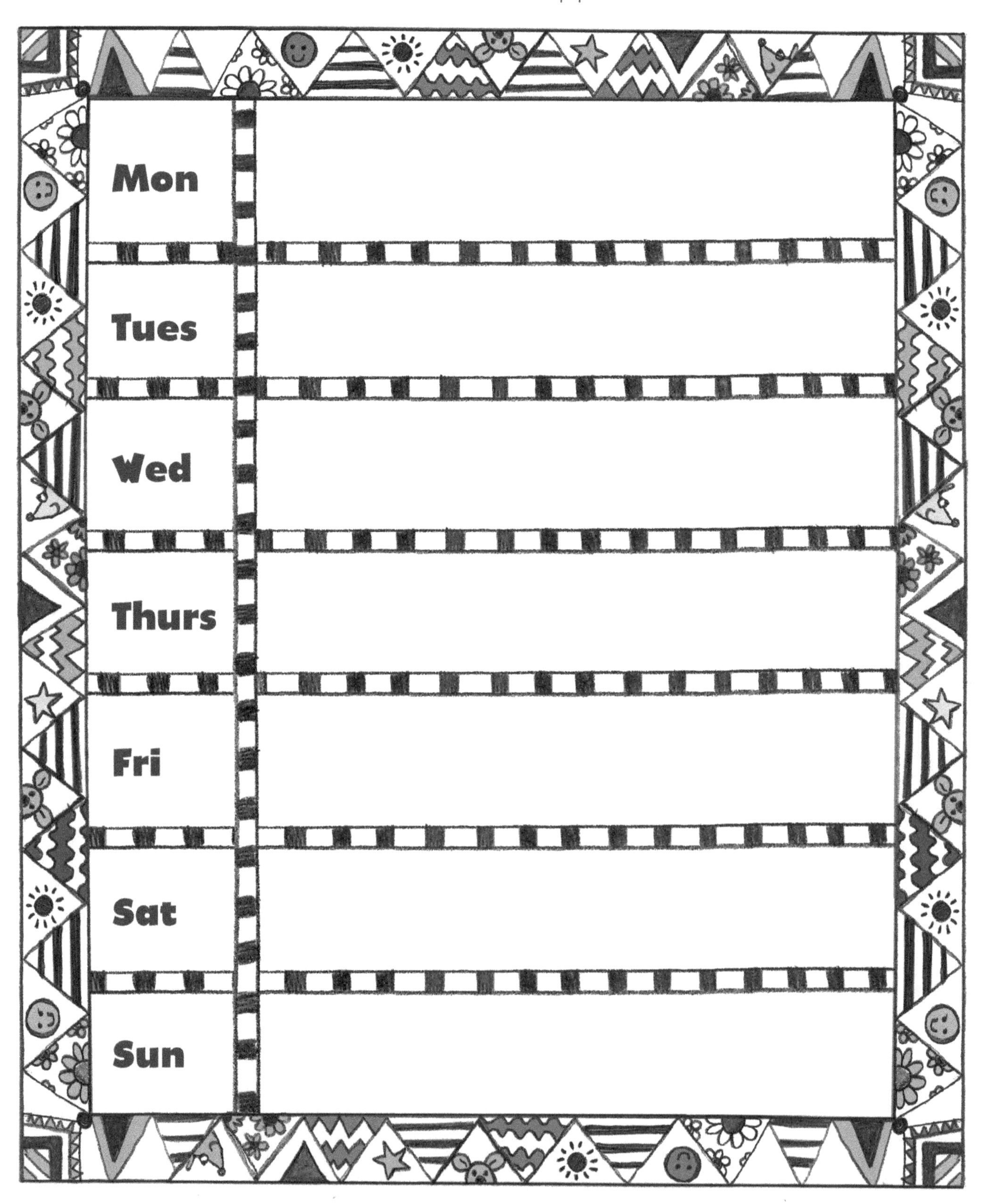

My Happiness Diary

Happy things happen every day!
Here are some that have happened to me...

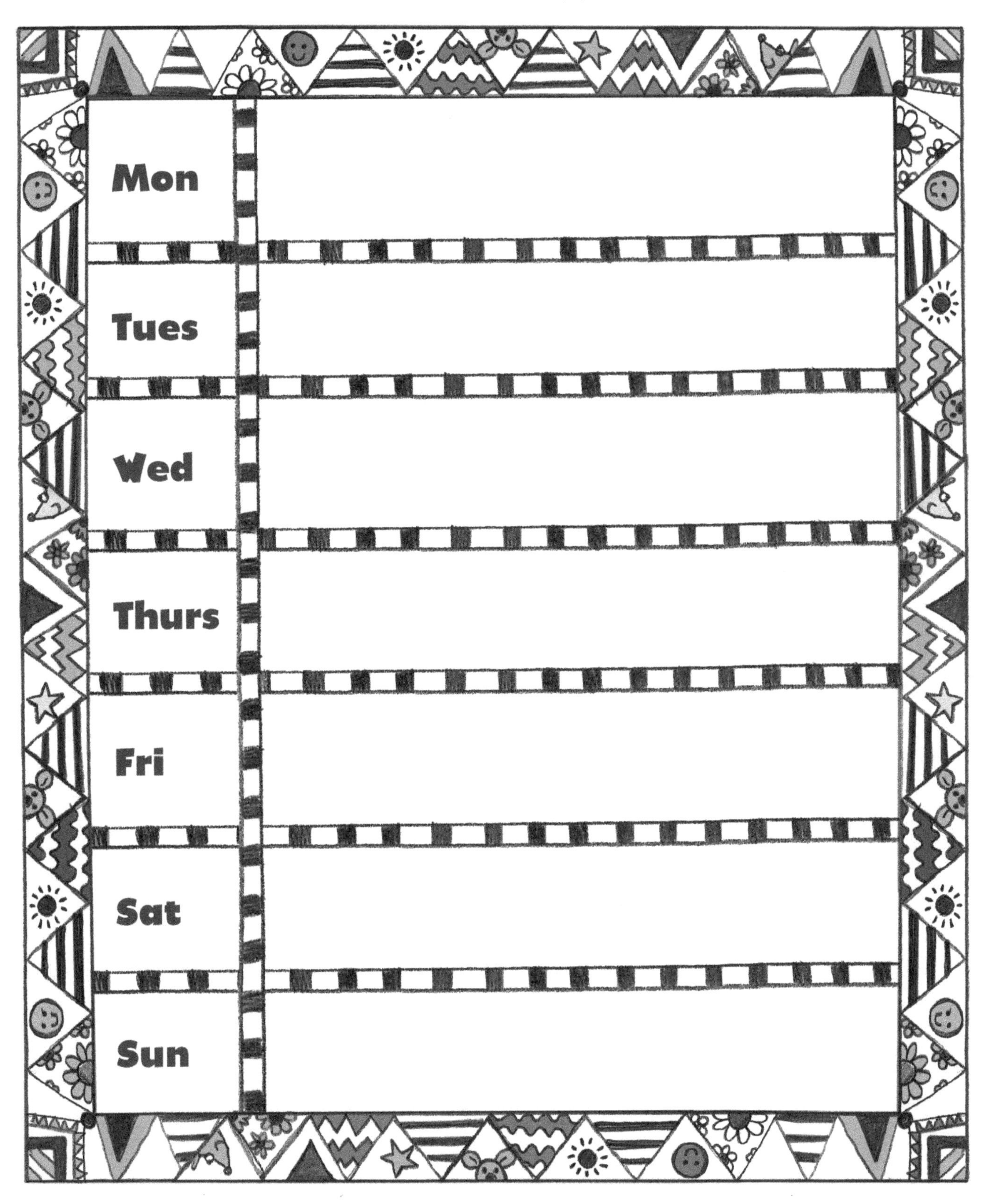

My Happiness Diary

Happy things happen every day!
Here are some that have happened to me...

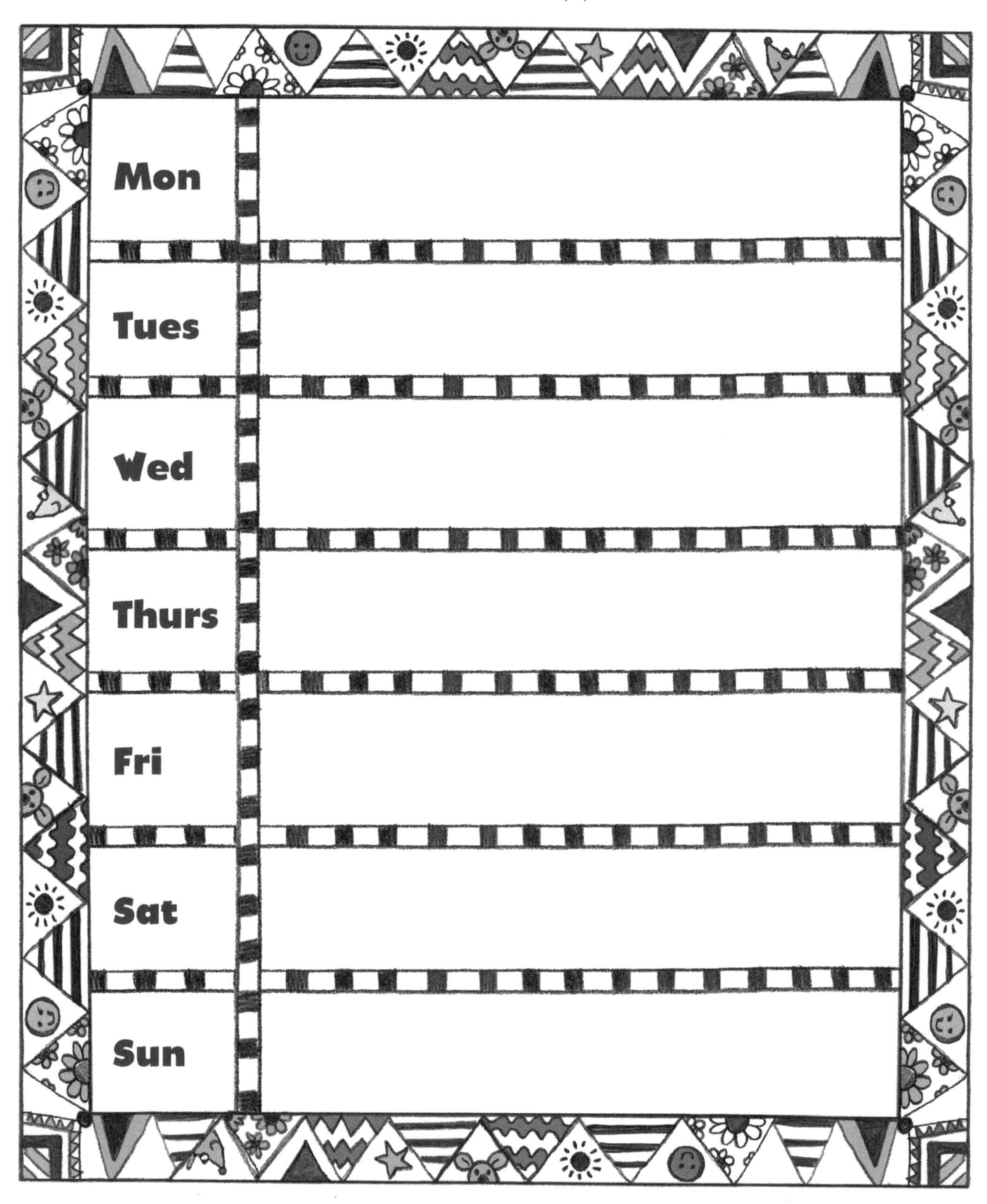

My Happiness Diary

Happy things happen every day!
Here are some that have happened to me...

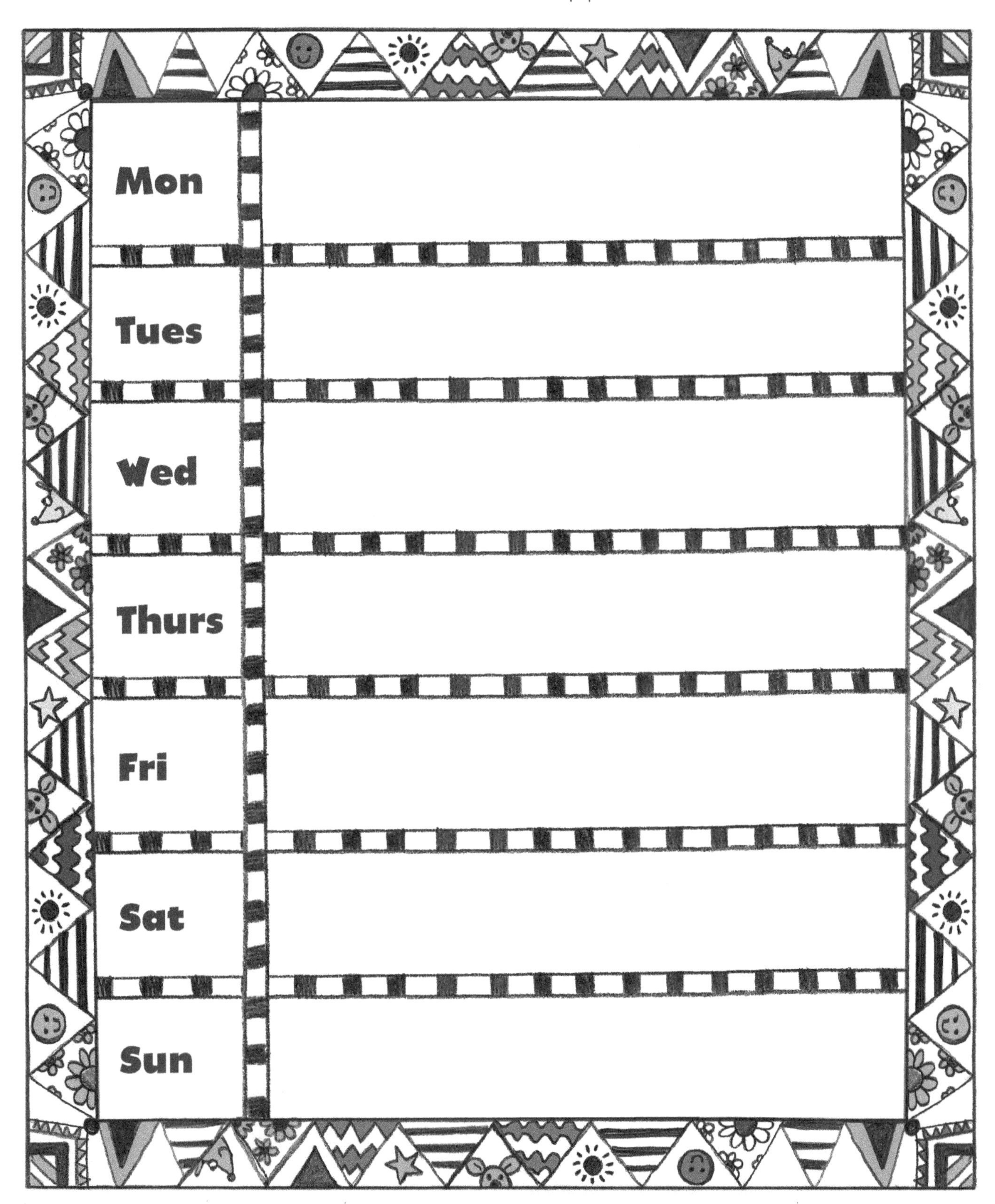

My Happiness Diary

Happy things happen every day!
Here are some that have happened to me...

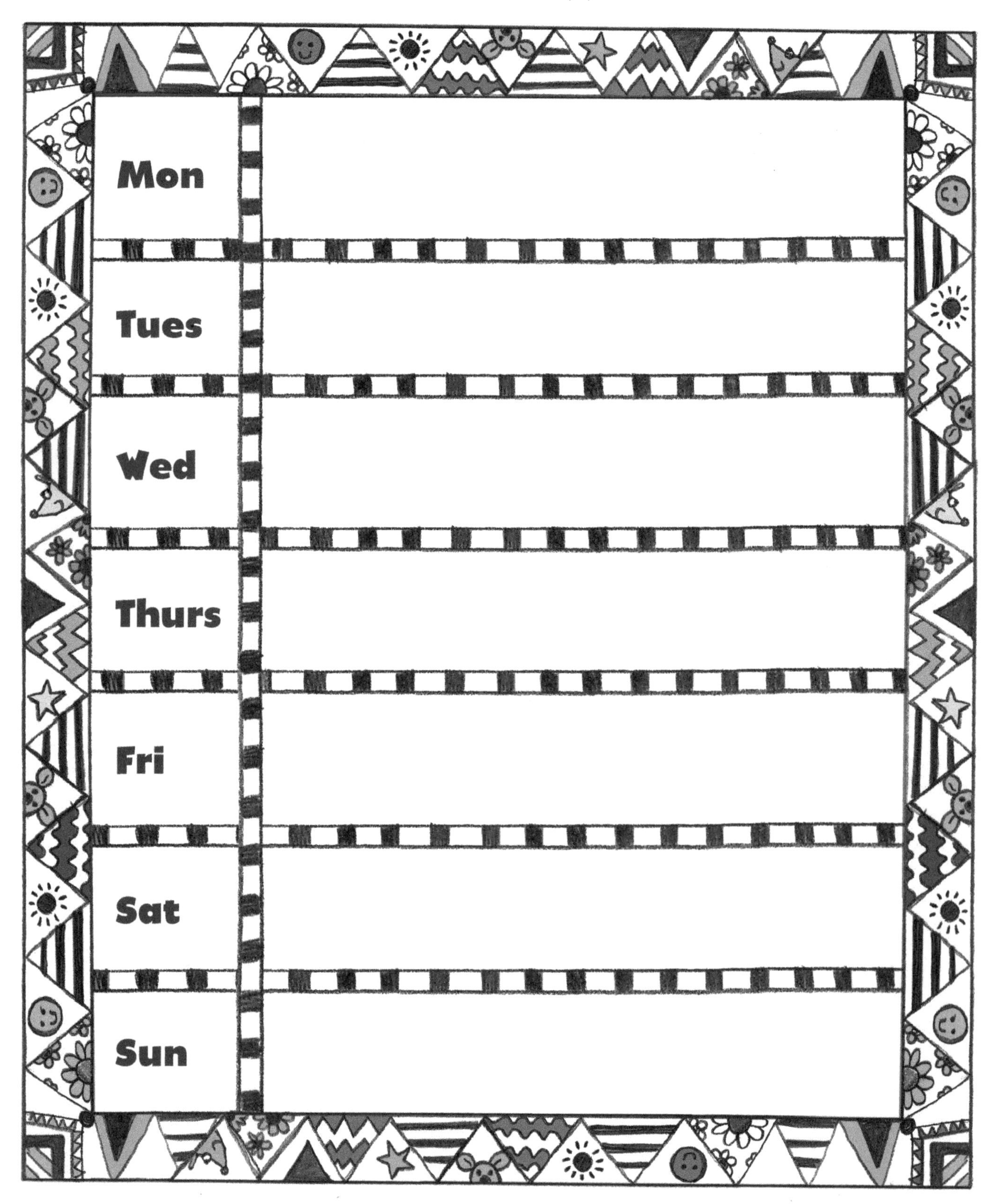